THE TEMPLES AND RITUAL

OF ASKLEPIOS

THE

TEMPLES AND RITUAL
OF ASKLEPIOS

AT EPIDAUROS AND ATHENS

TWO LECTURES DELIVERED AT THE ROYAL INSTITUTION OF GREAT BRITAIN

BY

RICHARD CATON, M.D., F.R.C.P.

HON. PHYSICIAN LIVERPOOL ROYAL INFIRMARY
EMERITUS PROFESSOR OF PHYSIOLOGY, UNIVERSITY COLLEGE, LIVERPOOL

WITH THIRTY FOUR ILLUSTRATIONS

SECOND EDITION

PRINTED AT THE UNIVERSITY PRESS OF LIVERPOOL

LONDON: C. J. CLAY AND SONS
CAMBRIDGE UNIVERSITY PRESS WAREHOUSE, AVE MARIA LANE
1900

CAMBRIDGE
UNIVERSITY PRESS

University Printing House, Cambridge CB2 8BS, United Kingdom

Published in the United States of America by Cambridge University Press, New York

Cambridge University Press is part of the University of Cambridge.

It furthers the University's mission by disseminating knowledge in the pursuit of education, learning and research at the highest international levels of excellence.

www.cambridge.org
Information on this title: www.cambridge.org/9781107656222

First published 1900
First paperback edition 2014

A catalogue record for this publication is available from the British Library

ISBN 978-1-107-65622-2 Paperback

PREFACE

Some apology is perhaps needed from one who can neither claim to be a classical scholar nor a professional archæologist in venturing upon the subject of these lectures.

Repeated visits to Greece and the Greek colonies during the past twenty years have enabled the author to observe, in their various stages, certain of the researches to be here briefly recounted. To him their interest appeared so considerable that it seemed probable the enquiry might be attractive to members of the medical profession generally, and perhaps also to other readers, from the side of the cult, if not from that of the classical archæologist.

The same motive explains the effort made to present a picture, in part hypothetical, of the ancient fabrics, and of the work carried on in them. More latitude in speculation in such a direction is perhaps allowable to one who traces the development of a cult, than to the scientific archæologist.

No originality is claimed in regard to the facts. Some of the sketches and restorations are original, and so are various theories or suggested explanations, such as that regarding the purpose of the Tholos and the Circular Pit at the Asklepieion ; the suggestion that the Square Building was a Prytaneion, where sacrificial banquets were held and

the perpetual fire maintained ; the theory that certain of the
buildings were hostels ; the conjecture regarding the selection
of sites for Greek Theatres, &c. Whether these are well-
founded or otherwise only time and further research can
decide.

The author desires to record his thanks to the learned
Oxford friend who edited and translated the inscription on
page 42, and who kindly pointed out various errors in the
first issue, also to Mr. Sampson, the librarian of University
College, Liverpool, for his highly valued advice and for his
kindness in reading the proofs of the present edition.

THE TEMPLES AND RITUAL OF
ASKLEPIOS

LECTURE I

LADIES AND GENTLEMEN,

You are aware that during the last twenty-five years
the energy and enthusiasm in archæological research of such
men as Dr. Schliemann have not merely thrown light on
historic and prehistoric Greece, but have also awakened a keener
enthusiasm among classical scholars and in those Societies which
in various countries are devoted to archæological investigation.
Even Governments have been influenced and induced to help
on the progress of these highly interesting studies. The
Germans have spent large sums in the excavation of Olympia
and Pergamos. The French government has wisely and
liberally incurred a considerable expenditure in the excavation
of Delphi and on other important works. The Greek Government, aided by members of the Greek Archæological Society,
has devoted money and an infinitude of labour to investigations
of the classic wealth of Greece and the Greek colonies.

In these three instances, although the amount paid may be
trivial when viewed in the national balance-sheet, its archæological equivalent is great. These three countries have not
only made the whole world their debtor by the liberality they
have displayed, but each has quickened and stimulated a taste
for learning and for art among its own people.

One or two other nationalities have had a share in the
progress made, though of a more private and individual kind.
The American School has explored the Argive Heræon and
certain other classical sites, and our own British School in
Athens, whose chief wealth has been the enthusiasm of its

members, has done much, when we consider the difficulties to be met and the lack of that sufficient pecuniary support with which other countries have endowed their representatives.

Although considerable interest is felt by the English public in regard to much of the work just referred to, one important field of investigation has remained comparatively unknown in this country—I mean the exploration of the shrines of Asklepios, the god of healing, at Epidauros and Athens, about which I am to have the honour of speaking to you. As the time allotted is brief, it is needful to avoid all prefatory remarks, and to restrict this paper almost entirely to a consideration of the new discoveries and to inferences from them. As a matter of fact, apart from the Hippocratic writings there is but scant information as to the sanitary and medical aspects of Greek life in ancient literature. Homer and Pindar have brief references to Epidauros and other sanctuaries of the god ; so also have Plato, Hippys of Regium, Strabo, and some of the dramatists, as Aristophanes, and certain of the late Greek writers, especially Pausanias. Under these circumstances most precious are the researches made by the spade.

The pioneer in this inquiry was M. Cavvadias, the eminent archæologist, Ephor of Antiquities and late Minister of Education in the Greek government. To him more than to any one else we owe the important additions lately made to this branch of archæology.

He worked in conjunction with the Greek Archæological Society, and was aided by M. Staïs, the Conservator of the National Museum. Herr Baunack and others helped to restore and decipher the hundreds of inscriptions which were found—a work of no small difficulty.

Various authorities more or less associated with the French School, such as M. Gérard, MM. Defrasse and Lechat, and Prof. Reinach ; Dr. Dörpfeld, Prof. Furtwängler, Herr Baunack, Dr. Köchler, and others associated with the German School, have had a share in the work or in recording its results.

Comparatively little has been done by the English, and only a limited amount of description has been published in our language. An interesting paper by Professor Percy Gardner, in his *New Chapters in Greek History*, some valuable references by Miss Jane Harrison and Mrs. Verrall in their *Mythology and Monuments of Ancient Athens*, the admirable notes in Mr.

Frazer's new edition of *Pausanias*, and one or two articles in American journals, such as the *American Antiquarian* and *Cornell Studies*, are among the chief.

For details of the work of the various writers *see* appended list of authorities consulted.

I have to express my acknowledgment to the authorities I have named, but chiefly to M. Cavvadias for his kindness in giving me special facilities in Greece, and for allowing me the use of some of his plates ; also to MM. Defrasse and Lechat, and to their publishers, who permit me to show you some of their beautiful restorations. Apart from these the lantern slides I shall show you are from photographs or sketches taken by myself on the scene of the various excavations or in museums.[1]

I. The Hieron of Epidauros

According to tradition, Asklepios, the son of Apollo and Koronis, was born in the Hieron valley, in the Argolic peninsula ; the place names still preserve the legend ; the hamlet of Koroni commemorates his mother, the hill Titthion owes its name to his having been there suckled by a goat, while on the opposite hill, Kynortion, stood the temple of the Maleatean Apollo.

The Hieron six miles from the town of Epidauros was the chief seat of the worship of Asklepios, though minor ones existed in Athens, at Delphi, Pergamos, Troizen, Kos, Trikke, and other places.

*Plate I is an outline restoration, representing some of the principal buildings in the Hieron.

I must warn the reader that this plan does not profess to be accurate. The structural detail of the buildings is always more or less conjectural, even their relative size and their distances from one another are only approximately correct. The object of the plan is to give a general idea of the arrangement of the chief buildings hitherto discovered, exclusive of the theatre. (It should be stated here that the numbers which follow refer to the illustrations, while the capital letters correspond with those on Plate I).

---

[1] About one-third of the lantern slides are here reproduced.

*available for download from www.cambridge.org/9781107656222

A represents the gateway or Propylæa (or perhaps temple of Hygieia) on the south of the precinct. Its close relation to the quadrangle *B* has caused some observers to suppose it was the entrance to *B* alone, but to the writer this seems improbable.

B is a large quadrangle about 250 feet square, reminding one of the Palæstra at Olympia. The central space was surrounded by small rooms and a colonnade; some of the columns of the latter remain, embedded in the later Roman brickwork of a music hall or Odeon, constructed within the quadrangle. Nine rows of seats and part of the stage of the Odeon still remain. The building has been supposed to be a gymnasium; but if so, must have ceased to be the scene of gymnastic exercises after the quadrangle was built upon in Roman times. Was it a hostel?

PLATE II—Restoration of East End of Temple of Asklepios
(Defrasse)

C represents the temple of Asklepios, the central shrine, a richly decorated and coloured doric building, erected in the fourth century B.C., the east end of which is shown in the accompanying restoration by Defrasse, Plate II. At the west and east gables were pediment groups representing a battle

PLATE III—Remains of Amazon from Pediment

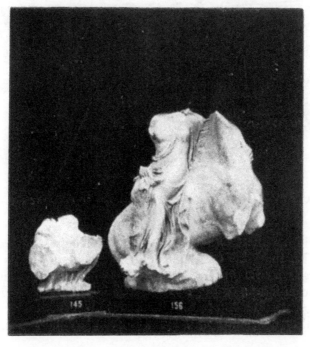

PLATE IV—Remains of a Nereid, one of the Acroteria

with Centaurs and a combat of Greeks and Amazons : one of
the latter is shown in Plate III ; together with acroteria, as in
Plate IV, which shows one of the two Nereids alighting
from horseback ; these stood on the two sides, while a central
winged victory occupied the apex of the gable.

A beautiful ivory door, which cost 3,000 drachmæ, closed
the sanctuary ; within, the cella was a single chamber ; there
was no opisthodomus.

Plate V, a restoration by M. Defrasse, represents the south
side of the temple, and also, towards the left, a part of the
Abaton.

PLATE V—Restoration of part of Abaton and of Temple of Asklepios
(Defrasse)

Within the temple stood, as shown in Defrasse's drawing,
Plate VI, the great chryselephantine statue of Asklepios made
by Thrasymedes of Paros, a work somewhat resembling the
Parthenon figure, or the vast Zeus of Olympia, or the Hera at
the Argive Heræon ; the flesh was ivory, the rest gold
splendidly enamelled in colours. So many small replicas of

this figure remain—sculptured copies found at Epidauros, or small representations on ancient coins—that by the aid of Pausanias' description M. Defrasse has doubtless reproduced the image with a near approach to accuracy.

The god was sitting on a throne, a large golden serpent rising up to his left hand ; on his right lay a dog, and in front was an altar.

PLATE VI—Restoration of chryselephantine figure of Asklepios
(Defrasse)

Gold and ivory were beautiful materials for the sculptor, though involving much difficulty when combined. The disappearance of all attempts at chryselephantine sculpture in modern times is perhaps due to this difficulty in production and to the cost, but probably more to the fact that the ivory usually tended to crack. The great figure of Athena in the Parthenon needed, we know, to be frequently moistened on its ivory surface with water. At Olympia, oil was applied to the great figure of Zeus, but curiously enough the Asklepios at

Epidauros needed neither. As the god of medicine, it may be supposed that he was able to preserve his own integument, but Pausanias tells us that a well, beneath the pavement of the temple, diffused sufficient moisture to prevent contraction and cracking of the ivory.[1]

On the throne were representations, doubtless in relief, of Bellerophon killing the Chimæra, and of Perseus with the head of the Medusa.

PLATE VII—BASE OF TEMPLE OF ASKLEPIOS

Plate VII. represents the remains of the temple as they exist to-day. Fragments of column, capital, pediment, &c., with pavements and bases of walls, render the hypothetical reconstruction of the building fairly easy.

D D in my first illustration is the Ionic portico or Abaton, a part of which is seen in Plates V. and X.; the western part is in two stories, the lower one being in the

[1] Montfaucon (L'Antiq. Explic. 1 ii 289) quotes a curious story to the effect that Dionysios, the Tyrant of Syracuse, visiting Epidauros, stole the massive golden beard from the figure of the god. He excused the theft on the ground that it was unseemly for Asklepios to wear a beard when his father Apollo had none !

basement. It is open on the south side ; a double colonnade supports the roof, the eaves of which, together with the walls and columns, showed colour decoration. This constituted the ward or sleeping place for the sick who were awaiting the miraculous interposition of the god. The Abaton was furnished with pallets, lamps, tables, altars, and probably curtains, the patients themselves supplying their own bed clothing. Other details of this building will be given in the next lecture. It may be added here that from one point of

PLATE VIII—Remains of East Abaton

view these remains are highly interesting, for they constitute the earliest known example of a Hospital Ward. There is reason to believe that institutions closely related to Infirmaries or Hospitals existed in Egypt many centuries earlier than the founding of the Hieron, but no structural trace of such a building has been discovered.

The back or north wall of the Abaton, the front or south line of Ionic columns and the central line of columns can be clearly made out from the remaining fragments.

Plate VIII shows these remains of the eastern part of the Abaton. The photograph unfortunately is defective, and it gives the idea that the remains are less considerable and important than they really are.

In Plate IX the remains of the lower story of the western part are shown. This photograph was taken from the top of the stairs leading down to the area-like court from which access was obtained to the lower story.

PLATE IX—Remains of lower story of West Abaton

The Tholos or Thymele, shown at *E* in Plate I and in the annexed restoration by Defrasse, Plate X, was probably the most beautiful circular temple that the Greeks ever built, far surpassing the Philippeion at Olympia. It was built in the fourth century B.C., by Polykleitos the younger, and took twenty-one years to build; externally it presented a beautiful doric colonnade, with peculiarly rich cornice, coloured. Within was a circle of sixteen graceful corinthian columns of marble; the wall and floor were also decorated with variously coloured marbles. Here were two celebrated paintings by Pausias, the

Greek artist ; the first represented Methe (drunkenness), a woman holding a large wine goblet to her lips, the glass of which was so painted that the face was seen through, or reflected in it.   The second, a picture of Eros (love) laying aside his bow and quiver and taking up his lyre, a less dangerous weapon.   Perhaps we may suppose that the painter here indicated the relation of Bacchus and Venus to the ailments which afflict mankind.   The scourges which we are told the gods make out of the pleasant vices of men doubtless often brought the wealthy Greek as a suppliant to Asklepios.

PLATE X—Restoration of Tholos   (Defrasse)

What was the purpose of the Tholos?   Defrasse and Lechat believe it was a drinking-fountain, a sort of pump-room, in which in old times a healing spring arose ; if so, we can imagine the gouty Athenian being sent here to drink large draughts from the holy spring, he envying meanwhile Methe and her occupation on the wall before him.   The foundations are curious, consisting of a series of circular walls forming a labyrinth, every part of which must necessarily be traversed by the explorer seeking the central space, Plate XI.

MM. Defrasse and Lechat think this singularly constructed basement was a water cistern from which the 'pump-room' above was supplied. The difficulties attending this rather attractive hypothesis are—(a) that the word 'Thymele' means a sacrificing place ; (b) Pausanias speaks of the Tholos and of the sacred well as though they were entirely distinct places ; (c) after careful search I can find no trace of a water conduit ; (d) the basement space, I may say confidently, was not cemented, either on wall or floor, as in all probability it would

PLATE XI—Foundation of Tholos

have been if to hold water. Not improbably the Tholos was employed for minor sacrifices, and perhaps the labyrinth below may have been associated with some mysterious Asklepian rite of which we are now ignorant ; e.g., the labyrinth may have been the home of the sacred serpents. We do not know what were the domestic economics of these creatures ; they, in an especial degree, were the incarnation of the god. They were treated by the sick with the utmost veneration ; perhaps this curious basement structure was their retreat, and conceivably the upper stage of the Tholos was employed for the offering of sacrifices to them as representatives of the god.   Perhaps the sacrificial cakes (πόπανα) were here offered to them.   An aperture in the floor may have been provided allowing the passage of the serpents from the labyrinth to the sacrificing place above.   We know that the sick were in the habit of

PLATE XII—Restoration of Temple of Artemis   (R. C.)

offering these cakes to the serpents as a matter of common usage.

Plate I, Letter *F.*   The Temple of Artemis is smaller than that of Asklepios (see Plate XII) ; the eaves were decorated by a rich cornice of sculptured heads of dogs, the attribute of Artemis-Hekate.   She, the sister of Apollo, was a divinity of healing and succour, the chaste moon goddess, who healed Æneas.   Acroteria of Victories decorated the eastern gable ;

within was a row of marble columns, and externally stood a triple figure of Artemis-Hekate, and an altar.

Letter *G* in Plate I shows the position of the grove, which probably extended also in the direction of the Tholos. *H* in the same plate shows the position of an altar which may have been sacred either to Asklepios or to Artemis. The letter *I* shows a foundation on which probably a much larger altar formerly stood ; it may have been that of Asklepios, on which possibly holocausts were offered. *J* represents the southern boundary of the precinct. *β* is thought to have been the shrine of the Ἐπιδόται or bountiful gods.

K in Plate I represents the square building which has occasioned much discussion. It contains the base of an altar surrounded by many bones of sacrificial animals and much ash, also fragments of bronze and earthenware, many of them bearing dedications to Apollo or Asklepios. Its period of erection seems to have been not later than the beginning of the fifth century B.C. It contained great numbers of statues and inscriptions. It may have been a house for priests or officials, or even a hostel, or possibly was the Prytaneion, on the altar of which burnt the perpetual fire ; no mention is, however, made of a Prytaneion in the inscriptions.

L in Plate I represents a large building, irregular, and of various date ; believed to have been the baths of Asklepios ; this building perhaps may have also contained the library, dedicated to the Maleatean Apollo and Asklepios, which one would think is likely to have been in some central position.

M in Plate I is intended to represent a rectangular building of which only small traces remain. Whether or not it was a definitely constructed quadrangle, such as I have drawn, may be uncertain. If it was, perhaps we have here the remains of one of the two gymnasia which the inscriptions tell us existed at the Hieron, or it may have contained baths.

N in the same plate is a restoration of the building with the four quadrangles, only lately excavated. It is the largest building yet discovered at the Hieron, being nearly 90 yards square. Each of the four quadrangles is surrounded by a number of rooms. In all there were between seventy and eighty of these apartments, each of which opened into its own quadrangle, so far as I could judge. A colonnade ran round the interior of each quadrangle. Query, what is it ?—a

gymnasium, a palæstra, a college for the priests, or a great
hostel? I confess the last-named seems the most probable.
When one considers the large number of the sick who came to
the Hieron, it is obvious that extensive accommodation must
have been provided for them somewhere. The two chambers
of the abaton could not have held more than 120 beds,
supposing these to have been placed in two rows; or if we
suppose the almost dark lower story of the western end to
have been a dormitory also, 180 would then have been the

PLATE XIII—North-Eastern Colonnade

greatest possible accommodation. This, if the extreme number
to be entertained, scarcely accords with the accounts given
by ancient writers of the multitudes who came for healing. to
the sanctuary. It appears likely, therefore, that this and other
undetermined buildings were hostels for the accommodation of
those whose ailments were slight or who were convalescent.

The remains of this curious structure are shown as seen
from a distance in Plate XVII below

O in Plate I is a Roman building. Cavvadias thinks that *a* is the temple of Asklepios and the Egyptian Apollo.

P is a building also of the Roman Period, and evidently contained baths. There are traces of a hypocaust. The remains of hot air or hot water pipes are abundant, and certain curious apse-like recesses in the walls, containing a seat and terminating below in a bath or deep basin, were evidently a form of sitzbath. When we remember that the French have lately discovered at Delphi no less than three extensive bathing

PLATE XIV—Figure of Aphrodite

establishments, adjacent to the walls of the precinct on the east, west, and south sides respectively, it is not surprising that we should find at least two such buildings at Epidauros. A part of this Roman bath-house is seen in the distance in Plate XIII.

Q in Plate I is a quadrangular building between the Temple of Artemis and the South Portal. Round three if not four of its sides were rooms, as in the case of the great four-quadrangle building ; many remains of columns are seen. Its purpose is doubtful. Probably it is the Colonnade of Kotys which Pausanias mentions. (It is to be hoped that no shrine of the dissolute Thracian goddess of that name existed here.)

This Colonnade of Kotys we know was originally built of sun-dried brick, and may perhaps originally have had wooden columns. Sun-dried brick, so common in many parts of Greece to-day, was often used in ancient times for important purposes, as, for example, in the building of the Heræon at Olympia. When this somewhat perishable material was covered with a fine hard cement, which resisted the heaviest rain, walls so constructed became wonderfully durable. The Colonnade of Kotys was rebuilt during Roman times. Some of the roof tiles discovered lately bear the name of Antoninus. Cavvadias suggests that the small temple γ is that of Themis.

R in Plate I is a colonnade which extended east and west nearly at right angles with the Roman Baths *P* described above. Plate XIII shows the remains of this colonnade, also a small open aqueduct with basins in its course about eleven yards apart. This small water channel reminds the visitor of a similar one existing in front of the Echo Colonnade at Olympia, the latter contains one or two basins like those shown in the plate. This view shows in the distance the Roman baths (*P*).

Adjoining this colonnade on the north-east is a large quadrangle *S*, formerly bordered on its four sides by columns. Its length east and west was about double its breadth north and south. Was this another hostel ?

T is believed by M. Cavvadias to be the Temple of Aphrodite, a Doric structure only excavated in 1892. An inscription discovered on the spot speaks of the sanctuary of Aphrodite ; not far from it was found a statue of the goddess in Parian marble, a most beautiful figure now preserved in the Museum at Athens. Plate XIV is an attempt to represent this figure as it now exists. The ancient cemetery of the Hieron was near the point marked ε in Plate I.

U in Plate I is an Ionic building, the present condition of which is shown in Plate XV. It may be a temple external to the precinct, or it may, as others suggest, be the Northern Propylæa or Ceremonial Gateway. The latter appears the more probable explanation ; by this entrance the pilgrims who came from the port of Epidaurus would approach the Sanctuary. Note the small well in the foreground.

V is a Roman building of unknown purpose, and *W*

represents a barrier which probably was the northern wall of the precinct. A wall protected the sacred enclosure on every side, "Τὸ δὲ ἱερὸν ἄλσος τοῦ Ἀσκληπιοῦ περιέχουσιν ὅροι πανταχόθεν,"* says Pausanias, but fully one-half of this barrier has yet to be found. It will be noted that, as at Olympia, many important buildings are external to the precinct.

Plate XVI represents a side view of the theatre (which is not shown in the outline plan Plate I).

PLATE XV—Northern Propylæa and Well

The Great Theatre situated to the south or ;the precinct was built about the year 450 B.C. by Polykleitos, the architect of the Tholos. Pausanias, who was a great traveller, tells us it was the most interesting of all the theatres existing in his time, and to-day any one who is familiar with the theatres of Greece and the Greek colonies will say that this is more impressive than any of the others. The Koilon or auditorium consisted of fifty-five rows of marble seats, with twenty-four lines of stairs. The space for the chorus is, according to the ancient system,

* Lib. II cap. xxvii § 1.

circular, and in the centre doubtless stood an altar of Bacchus. The stage was elevated nearly twelve feet, the proscenium being enriched by splendid sculpture. The acoustics of the theatre are perfect ; a sound little louder than a whisper uttered on the stage can be heard in every part. The theatre is so placed on the slope of Kynortion that the occupants of the major part of the auditorium had a charming view (over the top of the stage) of the mountains to the north and of the whole range of beautiful buildings of the Hieron.

PLATE XVI—Theatre

Plate XVII represents the view taken from the top row of seats. Note the circular chorus space, the remains of the "four quadrangle building," and glimpses of the Hieron beyond. While witnessing here the sublime tragedies of Æschylus or Sophocles, or such a comedy as the *Plutus* of Aristophanes (in which, as you will remember, great fun is made at the expense of Asklepios and his priests), the contrast afforded by glancing from the stage to the blues and purples of the mountains, the verdancy of the grove, and the beautiful forms and colours of the group of temples would be most pleasing. The Greeks were acute in perceiving and taking advantage of subtle sources of pleasure like this, and I believe that the sites of many of their theatres were chosen so as to secure for the audience this double pleasure. The Theatre of Delphi is a conspicuous example of this provision, as also is that of Tauromena. This theatre has been said to seat 12,000 spectators ; according to my own rough computation, it unquestionably will hold over 9,000 without crowding.

PLATE XVII—View of Theatre from top row of seats, ruins of the "four quadrangle building" in the distance

Before quitting this theatre it may be remarked that Dr. Dörpfeld's interesting and attractive theory of the occupancy of orchestra and stage equally by the players in a Greek drama, is difficult of application in this individual case, in consequence of the great difference in level—eleven or twelve feet—between the two. So great a disparity of surface would, as most people think, seriously interfere with the unity of the representation, even if flights of steps connected orchestra and stage.

X in Plate I represents part of the Stadium, which is about six hundred feet long. Here are remains of at least fifteen rows of marble seats. Probably foot races took place here as well as other forms of athletic exercise. All the maps of the Hieron represent the eastern end of the Stadium as semicircular, but so far as one can judge, the latest excavations indicate that it was square, and therefore I have so represented it.

PLATE XVIII—East end of Stadium

Assuming that the fifteen rows of seats extended from end to end on each side, and allowing a foot and a half for each person, the Stadium would seat twelve thousand spectators on its two sides, without computing the seats at the ends.

Plate XVIII represents the excavation at the end adjacent to the Hieron. *Y* in Plate I (shown also in Plate XVIII) is either the starting place or the goal. *Z* is a subterranean passage probably communicating with the precinct.

An inscription (found in 1896) mentioned by Mr. Frazer, shows that a hippodrome also existed at the Hieron.

On Mount Kynortion, some distance south of the great theatre, stood the temple of the Maleatean Apollo. The remains are so fragmentary that it is difficult to devise a conjectural restoration.

II. The Asklepieion at Athens.

Before saying anything about the ritual and the treatment of the sick at the Hieron, it will be well to turn to the Asklepieion at Athens, and examine briefly the structural

PLATE XIX--Portico of Eumenes and Acropolis

arrangements there. Situated on the south side of the Acropolis, at an elevation of perhaps eighty feet above the plain, adjoining on the east the theatre of Dionysus, the locality was probably as healthy as any the immediate neighbourhood of Athens could supply. The heat no doubt was great in summer, but we may conclude that a grove of large trees afforded grateful shade to the sick.

Plate XIX represents the remains of the Stoa or Portico of Eumenes (so called) lying to the south of the Acropolis. To the extreme left is seen the temple of the Nike Apteros, and on

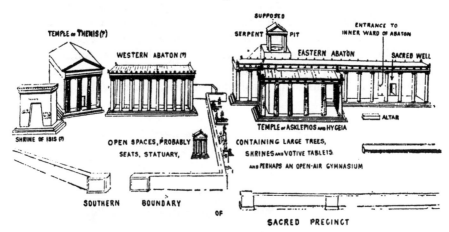

PLATE XX—Attempt at an Outline Restoration of the Asklepieion at Athens (R. C.)

PLATE XXI—Remains of Asklepieion from the West

the summit of the Akropolis the Parthenon.   Between the Stoa
and the rock of the Akropolis is situated the Asklepieion.   The
accompanying outline plan, No. XX, is an attempt to give
some idea of the arrangement of buildings within the precinct.
The buildings were to a certain extent an imitation, on a smaller
scale, and on a limited area, of those at the Hieron of
Epidauros.   Remains of what were probably a temple of
Asklepios and Hygieia, of doric architecture, also a supposed
temple of Themis, and a shrine of Isis, exist, while smaller

PLATE XXII—Remains of Asklepieion from the East

shrines of Serapis, Kore, Hypnos, Herakles, Panakia, Demeter,
and other divinities have left no distinct traces.   There are
considerable remains of a large eastern portico or abaton of
pentelic marble, from which is reached a circular chamber in
the rock containing the sacred well.   Some of the masonry
here seems to me to be of late Roman date.

Plate XXI represents the Asklepieion as seen from the
western end, and plate XXII from the east.   The building

inscribed "western abaton" in plan No. XX may have been a supplementary abaton or a priest's house or a covered gymnasium. A grove existed, perhaps occupying the space between the Stoa of Eumenes and the temples, or situated in a large vacant space to the west.

On an elevation above and close to the abaton is a curious well-like structure, surrounded by marble columns, which perhaps was the serpent pit.

PLATE XXIII—Supposed Serpent Pit and remains of Marbled Columns round it

Plate No. XXIII represents the remains of this curious and mysterious structure. I examined the masonry carefully to see if a direct communication between this supposed snake pit and the abaton could be traced, but failed to find it. If the purpose of the Tholos at Epidauros is that suggested above, viz., a place of sacrifice to the sacred serpents, may we not have here also the remains of a Tholos or Thymele on a small scale ? Possibly the four marble bases are those of columns surrounding an altar to which the serpents ascended from their pit beneath, to receive the sacrificial cakes of the worshippers, who themselves stood beneath a roof carried by these columns. This of course is a mere hypothesis.

The grove contained great numbers of statues, busts, ex-votos, and inscriptions. The theatre of Dionysos close at hand was doubtless frequented by the sick as a diversion. The stall occupied by the priest of Asklepios, with his name on it, is still in excellent preservation, as seen in plate XXIV. He sat in the first rank, in a most honoured position, with his back to the setting sun, next to the priest of the Muses. The Panathenaic stadium, three-quarters of a mile away, doubtless was also frequently visited by the convalescents from the Asklepieion.

PLATE XXIV—Seats of Priests of Asklepios and of the Muses in the Theatre

LECTURE II

WE now pass on to consider the ritual of the Asklepian shrines and the accommodation and treatment of the sick who frequented them.

It is convenient, first, to consider the Hierarchy. They consisted of the Hiereus or Hierophant, the priest, who was the head official. He was appointed annually, and he appears to have been frequently re-elected. From the Athenian inscriptions we know that sometimes he was a physician, sometimes not; so also it was with the subordinate officials. The priest was the general administrator, and had a share in the financial government of the temple. The Dadouchoi, or torch-bearers, were probably subordinate priests; the Pyrophoroi, or fire-carriers, among other functions, lighted the sacred fire on the altars; the Nakoroi or Zakoroi, whose duties in the temple are uncertain, sometimes were physicians; the Kleidouchoi, or key-bearers, who perhaps were originally a class of superior door porters, but who appear later to have assumed priestly functions; the Hieromnemones seem to have had purely secular duties, and in common with the Hiereus had charge of all receipts and payments; all were under the rule of the Boule of Epidauros. The Kanephoroi (or basket-bearers) and the Arrephoroi (or carriers of mysteries or holy things) were priestesses. We read in some of the inscriptions of servants or attendants who ministered to the sick, and carried those who were unable to walk. Did these women in any degree act as nurses? It is possible, but no definite information on the subject is given.

There were certain officials, also, who attended to the sacred dogs; the serpents are not thus far known to have had such guardians. We read also of bath attendants.

There was also a special religious society termed the Asklepiastai.

Turning now from the priests to the suppliants: these, we find, came from all parts of the Greek world, and from what ancient writers tell us their numbers appear to have been great. Where were they housed? Some, of course, dwelt in the abaton, the women probably in one part and the men in another, for a wall divided the East from the West abaton; but, as I have already pointed out, not more than 120 could find beds there at a time; perhaps the invalid was only housed there at first, and when he began to improve was drafted off to a hostel. Assuming that all the buildings which I have suggested to be hostels were such, they could not accommodate more than some four or five hundred patients. Perhaps we may assume that such was the usual number attending at ordinary times, while at the great festivals many thousands assembled. Whether this large number were lodged in tents or temporary wooden buildings, or otherwise, is uncertain.

Probably multitudes of vigorous and able-bodied persons came to the festivals, and many of them may have been lodged six miles away at the town of Epidauros, or in villages or hamlets adjacent. The ten or twelve thousand who filled the Theatre or the Stadium cannot have been exclusively sick people. It seems probable that numbers of athletes and multitudes of Greeks who merely wanted a holiday and a little excitement came to the Megala Asklepieia as they came to the Isthmian or the Olympic games. Setting aside, therefore, all visitors of this class, who probably brought gains to the Sanctuary, and for whom accordingly space was provided in the Theatre, Stadium, and Hippodrome, I pass on to consider the suppliants proper.

The patient on arrival probably had an interview with the priest or other official, and arranged about his accommodation with one of the Hieromnemones, or other secular person. He performs certain rites, bathes in the sacred fountain, and offers sacrifices under the direction of the Pyrophoros; the poor man gives his cake only, the rich his sheep, pig, or goat, or other offering in addition. The votive tablets frequently show the cakes (πόπανα) being presented, or the sheep, pig, or other animal. Where the ceremonial purification took place is uncertain. A deep well exists in the eastern abaton. A stone dropped struck the water in a fraction over three seconds, as I found after repeated trials. The well is therefore over 144 feet deep. Possibly the water used in the ritual was derived hence, but more probably the place of purification has yet to be found. "Only pure souls may enter here," was inscribed over the entrance of the temple of Asklepios.

Pausanias speaks of a fountain beautifully roofed and decorated, "κρήνη τῷ τε ὀρόφῳ καὶ κόσμῳ τῷ λοιπῷ θέας ἀξία."* Can this have been the bath of Asklepios marked **L** in my plan? Traces of a large basin remain there.

* Lib. II cap. xxvii § 5.

When night comes the sick man brings his bed-clothing into the abaton, and reposes on his pallet, putting usually some small gift on the table or altar. The Nakoroi having come round to light the sacred lamps, the priest enters and recites the evening prayers to the god, entreating divine help and divine enlightenment for all the sick assembled there; he then collects the gifts which had been deposited on altars and tables; later the Nakoroi enter, put out the lights, enjoin silence, and command everyone to fall asleep and to hope for guiding visions from the god. The abaton was a lofty and airy sleeping chamber, its southern side being an open colonnade. It is singularly like the 'shelter balcony' or *Liegehalle*, now used in treating phthisis. This provision of abundance of pure fresh air for the sick by day and night, which is so beneficial now, was undoubtedly so then also, and probably brought much credit to the god and his shrine.

According to the inscriptions the god frequently appeared in person, or in visions, speaking to the sick man or woman concerning their ailments. Whether these visitations were merely hallucinations in individuals whose imaginations had been excited, or whether some priest in the dim light, accompanied by a serpent, acted the part of Asklepios; whether the patient was put under the influence of opium or some other drug provocative of dreams; or whether, by some acoustic trick, the priests caused the sick to hear spoken words which they attributed to the deity, it is difficult now to say.

The valley of the Hieron was the habitat of a large yellow serpent, perfectly harmless, and susceptible, like most snakes, of domestication. Pausanias tells us it is found in the Epidaurian country alone. I am afraid it is now extinct, though it has been seen during the present century. A number of these creatures dwelt in the sanctuary, perhaps in the vaults of the Tholos. They were reverenced as the incarnation of the god. The sick were delighted and encouraged when one of these creatures approached them, and were in the habit of feeding them with cakes. The serpents seem to have been trained to lick with their forked tongue any ailing part. The dog also was sacred to Asklepios, and the temple dogs in like manner were trained to lick any injured or painful region of the body.

It will be remembered that in the *Plutus* of Aristophanes, the blind Plutus enters the abaton of the Asklepieion at Athens in order to be cured. Asklepios with his daughters,

Iaso and Panakeia, appear in person ; they whistle to the sacred
serpents, which at once approach, lick the blind eyes, and
vision is restored.

In the accompanying sketch of the abaton, Plate XXV, a
miracle is in progress in the foreground.   A lame man comes

PLATE XXV—RESTORATION OF THE INTERIOR OF THE ABATON AT EPIDAUROS
PATIENT SACRIFICING AND HAVING INJURED LEG LICKED BY THE SACRED SERPENT   (R.C.)

to the altar, he offers his sacrifice, the Pyrophoros lights the
sacred flame, the Dadouchos or Nakoros enjoins silence while
the holy serpent licks the affected part.   The abaton is nearly

empty, as it is the daytime, but one or two bedridden patients watch the miracle with interest.

In the inscriptions the phrase ἰάσατο τῇ γλώσσῃ, referring to the serpent, is met with, and also in reference to the dogs κύων τῶν ἱαρῶν ἐθεράπευσε τῇ γλώσσῃ.

Many of the *malades imaginaires*, who to this day are the support of the quack, and a cause of embarrassment and difficulty to the scientific physician—who desires above all things to be honest—doubtless visited Epidauros.

PLATE XXVI—HEAD OF ASKLEPIOS

The priest wearing the holy chaplet would take such a person (as probably he took all suppliants) into the temple, and cause him to present himself before the image of the god ; libations were poured, prayers and sacrifices offered, and rites of an impressive kind enacted. Hymns and pæans were sung to the music of the double flute. The sick man was caused to lay his hand solemnly and reverently on the altar of the god, and then on the part of his own body presumed to be affected ; if there were really nothing the matter, he was proclaimed to be miraculously cured by the god, and doubtless his imagination was so impressed that he often himself believed in the cure.

If the patient were young, sacrifices were doubtless offered at the shrine of Artemis-Hekate, and perhaps in all cases the procession of priests and suppliants visited the Tholos (which you remember was the Thymele or sacrificing place) and offered sacrifices there perhaps to the serpent, the incarnation of the god of healing ; or the train of votaries ascended Mount Kynortion to the shrine of the great Apollo.

PLATE XXVII—Asklepios with Serpent.

The suppliants spent the day in rest or exercise, as was most agreeable to them. It must be remembered that the precinct was as beautiful as the noblest works of Greek art could make it ; moreover large and lofty trees formed a shady grove, protecting from the sun's heat, while the soft breeze and the sweet pure air of the mountains formed in themselves a potent agency for the restoration of health. The patient had much around him to please and interest—beautiful buildings, rich with sculpture and with colour, statuary figures and groups representing Asklepios and other divinities or subjects from the old Greek mythology in marble and bronze.

Plate XXVI represents a head of Asklepios (from the Asklepieion at the Piræus), to which the genius of the sculptor has given an expression of sorrow and sympathy, as though the god were grieving over the sufferings of mankind.

Plate XXVII shows a full-length figure of the god, found at Epidauros, accompanied as usual by the serpent. Artistic reliefs, hermæ, and full-length figures of noted priests and physicians, and of individuals eminent in art, philosophy,

PLATE XXVIII—Shelter-seat

literature, or history ; also ex-votos, stelæ, and tablets recording the marvellous cures effected by the god, coloured bas-reliefs, encaustic paintings, shrines, exedræ, decorative vases and fountains, beautified and added interest to the precinct.

Shelter-seats, arranged in semicircles, of beautiful white marble, were so placed as to avoid sun or wind ; they were convenient for converse, or for listening to a reader or a musician.

Plates XXVIII and XXIX represent the remains of two of these seats at the Hieron ; close to the former is seen a large pedestal on which probably an equestrian statue formerly stood.

Many shrines and chapels to subsidiary deities existed, as, for example, to Hygieia, Themis, the Egyptian Apollo, Helios, Selene, Epione (the wife of Asklepios), Zeus, Poseidon, Minerva, Hera, Demeter and other Eleusinian deities, Dikaiosyne, Lato, Hypnos, Eileithyia, and others not as yet identified. The diminutive figure of Telesphoros, in his capacity of god of

PLATE XXIX—Shelter-seat

Convalescence, is not seen here so often along with Asklepios on ex-votos and coins, as at Pergamos and some other Temples.

Plate XXX represents a number of small figures of Hygieia and of Asklepios from the Hieron.

Every devout Greek who came as a suppliant to Asklepios would find here also a shrine of his own favourite deity.

To those who had been initiated at Eleusis, and whose advanced age or incurable sickness gave little prospect of life, the calm and dignified forms of Demeter, Persephone, and Iakchos would suggest patience and the hope of a pure spiritual after-life, free from all bodily infirmity, "for the Greek or Roman heart . . was as full, in many cases fuller, of the hope of immortality than our own."*

Those of the sick who were not too ill, would ascend the hill of Kynortion to visit the temple of Apollo, or climb the neighbouring hill of Titthion, sacred to the infancy of Asklepios. Others would engage in the exercises of the gymnasium or the

PLATE XXX—Figures of Asklepios and Hygieia

stadium ; if unable to participate in these more active pursuits, they would become spectators of them. The comedies or tragedies played in the theatre would often so immerse the audience in merriment or pathos as to banish for the time individual troubles ; both priest and patient attended them constantly. Music, the singing of Orpheic hymns, religious dances, processions, and festivals would vary the interest and occupations of the day. The studious man could occupy himself with manuscripts from the library, and, reposing in the

* Modern Painters, V, Part ix, Ch. 5, § 3.

shelter-seats, would dream over history, plays, or poetry. The solemn rites of the temple, the sacrifices, the study of the multitudinous tablets, would all tend to a calm and hopeful condition of mind, eminently helpful to recovery from slight forms of illness, even though no direct medical treatment were pursued.

In earlier times it seems as though the health-restoring influence of the shrines was thought to be wholly miraculous, with but small aid or none from art : the god alone achieved all. The more ancient inscriptions contain childishly absurd reports of miraculous cures.

The ruling idea was that the deity appeared to the sick man in the abaton, applied some medicament, performed some operation, or instructed the dreaming patient to carry out some sanative action when he awoke. The frauds of the god or his priest were so outrageous that some of the old Greeks seem almost to have equalled in folly and credulity the moderns, who readily buy soap or pills on no other warranty than the advertisements of a lying and interested vendor.

On the walls of the eastern abaton were fixed two large stone tablets, bearing the title, "Cures by Apollo and Asklepios." Most of the fragments of these tablets have been recovered, pieced together, and deciphered by M. Cavvadias and other learned palæographers. The following are a few extracts :—

Line 72 of the first tablet in the abaton.—A man who had only one eye is visited by the god in the abaton during the night. The god applies an ointment to the empty orbit. On awaking, the man finds he has two sound eyes.

Line 125.—Thyson of Hermione is blind of both eyes ; a temple dog licks the organs and he immediately regains his sight.

Line 107.—Hermodicos of Lampsacus comes to the Hieron in a paralyzed condition. As he sleeps in the abaton the god tells him to rise, to walk outside the precinct, and carry back into it the largest stone he can find. He does so, and brings in a stone so heavy that no other man can lift it, and the stone, as the inscription says, still lies before the abaton. The same stone (probably) lies there to-day, and the visitor may yet in vain emulate the feat of Hermodicos. It will be recognised in the illustration, Plate XXXI, by the hole cut in it to put the hands in.

Line 113.—A man had his foot lacerated by the bite of a

wild beast; he is in much pain; the servants of the abaton carry him outside during the daytime; as he is waiting to be healed a serpent follows him, licks his foot, and he is at once cured.

Line 122.—Heraieus of Mytilene has no hair on his head; he asks the god to make it grow again. Asklepios applies an ointment, and next morning the hair has grown thickly over his scalp. (Unfortunately Asklepios omitted to write down the prescription for the benefit of those in like case in the future!)

PLATE XXXI—THE STONE MIRACULOUSLY CARRIED BY THE
PARALYZED HERMODICOS

At line 48 begins a story containing a moral which the priests may have thought it desirable to impress upon their visitors :—

Pandaros comes all the way from Thessaly in order to have a disfiguring eruption or branding mark on his forehead cured; he is quickly made well. Returning to Thessaly his cure is observed by his neighbour Echedoros, who has a similar, but slighter, eruption on the face. He also goes to Hieron, carrying with him a sum of money sent to the god by the grateful Pandaros. Echedoros contemplates retaining this money himself; he consults the god about his own case, and in answer to a question states that he has brought no gift from Pandaros. On rising in the morning he finds that, instead of having his skin disease cured, that of Pandaros has been added to it.

Line 96.—A man from Toronœa is so unfortunate as not to be in the good graces of his stepmother; she introduces a number of leeches into the wine he drinks. Being of a submissive and confiding temperament, he swallows the beverage unsuspectingly, but the results are so serious that he is obliged to visit the god. Asklepios cuts open his chest with a knife, removes the leeches, sews up the chest again, and the patient returns home next day.

From other inscriptions we find that Asklepios treats dropsy surgically, in a simple but heroic manner; he first cuts off the patient's head, then holds him up by the heels; the fluid all runs out. He then puts the patient's head on again, and the case terminates happily.

These, I think, are a sufficient sample of the preposterous stories of cures which the god was reported to have performed in early times.

It is quite clear that the absolute liking which many men and women have for the charlatan, and for deception, their appetites for the marvellous and incredible in all medical matters, existed as strongly among the Greeks as among ourselves, though the superstitious beliefs and the ignorance of science prevailing in those times rendered such folly more excusable than it is now.

In later times it seems clear that superstition and deception had a less share, and art a larger one, in the work of healing at Hieron. Probably among the acute citizens of Athens, at no period were the frauds of the god so outrageous as in the early times at Hieron. We find the priests prescribing many things that were prudent and judicious; diet of a plain and simple character, hot and cold baths, poulticing for certain chest ailments, and a variety of medicaments—hemlock juice, oxide of iron, hellebore, squills, lime-water, and drugs for the allaying of pain—are incidentally mentioned. Water was used extensively both internally and externally; active gymnastic exercise, riding, friction of the skin, a sort of massage, and counter-irritation.

The tablet of Apellas of Idria tells us that when visiting the Hieron on account of frequent illness and severe indigestion, the god or his priests ordered a diet of bread and curdled milk, with parsley and lettuce, lemons boiled in water, also milk and honey.   Apellas being an irascible person, the god ordered careful avoidance of the emotion of anger, and desired him to run and swing in the gymnasium, and use vigorous friction and counter-irritation to the surface of the body.   Probably Apellas was a wealthy and luxurious city-dweller, who took too much food and Chian wine, and who suffered, as many in that age did, from gout.   He is eventually cured, and erects a tablet to show his gratitude.

Here is the invocation of another sufferer coming to the Hieron : "O blessed Asklepios, god of healing, it is thanks to thy skill that Diophantes hopes to be relieved from his incurable and horrible gout, no longer to move like a crab, no longer to walk upon thorns, but to have a sound foot as thou hast decreed." It would have been interesting to know how far Diophantes' hopes were realized.   If they met with disappointment, he may have regretted putting up the tablet at so early a stage.

There can be little doubt that many of the sick benefited greatly by the rest, the pure air, the simple diet, the sources of mental interest, the baths, exercise, massage, and friction, and in later days by the actual medical treatment adopted. Surgical treatment was also employed, for we find marble reliefs of surgical instruments.

Not infrequently it would happen that persons with real or with incurable diseases came to Hieron and got worse, notwithstanding their sacrifices and petitions to the god.   How the priests excused the impotency of their deity on these occasions we do not know ; perhaps some lack of merit, purity, or sanctity in the individual may have been imputed.   We know that in some cases the honour of Asklepios was saved by sending the unfortunate invalid to some distant shrine ; but of course it happened that in some instances the patient died while at the Hieron.   Now, according to the religion of the Greeks, two events were considered to desecrate in the most dreadful manner any hallowed precinct — namely, birth and death ; neither of these must occur within any sacred enclosure.

While the sick probably met with considerable kindliness, humanity, and real help at these shrines, and much actual benefit resulted, notwithstanding the superstition on which all

was based, still, in this one respect Greek tradition and ceremonial were a cause of the most gross inhumanity. The
unhappy visitant whose vital powers were finally declining was
received and domiciled in the abaton, but when he failed to
improve, and was seen by the priests and attendants to be
obviously dying, instead of being tenderly nursed and soothed,
he was removed from his couch, dragged across the precinct to
the nearest gate, expelled, and left to die on the hillside
unhelped and untended. Asklepios had rejected him, and no
priest or minister of the god must defile himself by any deal-
ings with death. One cannot but hope that the sympathy and
humanity which exist naturally in the hearts of most men and
of all women, found some means of helping these unhappy
beings, and that when death seemed probable such sufferers
were conveyed to a hostel outside the precinct, and allowed to
die in peace there. A like superstition existed regarding birth.
Many a poor woman who was anticipating maternity, and who
had been hoping for relief from some ordinary ailment, was
suddenly and mercilessly expelled from the precinct at the
moment when she needed help and comfort most.

Not until the time of the Antonines was any definite
provision made for these two classes of sufferers. Either
Antoninus Pius or Marcus Aurelius erected outside the precinct
a home for the dying, and a sort of maternity hospital.
Doubtless some of the ruins dating from the Roman period,
which are at present unidentified, subserved these two purposes.

As yet nothing has been said about the commissariat
arrangements of the Hieron. It is probable that several
hundred persons habitually resided there, if we include the sick,
the convalescents, the priests, officials, and servants, while on
the occasion of the great festivals the number rose to at least
ten or twelve thousand. What arrangements were made for
the dieting of all these? Where were the storehouses, the
kitchen and the "deipneterion," or dining-room, if any such
existed?

Probably the diet of the poorer patients may have consisted
largely of the barley-meal paste, the "maza" eaten with certain
inexpensive vegetables. This would require little preparation.
Among the well-to-do patients, however, who were numerous,
the meals would be more formal and would need more care in
preparation. In early times the "ariston" formed the breakfast,
and was eaten at sunrise. In later times this meal was moved

on to the middle of the day, and the "acratisma," consisting merely of bread dipped in unmixed wine, was eaten at an early hour. The mid-day meal in later times consisted of various warm dishes needing the art of the cook, and the principal meal, the "deipnon," which was still more elaborate, was just before sunset. Where the preparation and the consumption of these meals took place it is difficult to say.

The lower story of the western abaton may have been a storehouse, or possibly a kitchen. It must be remembered that the main part of the flesh of the animals presented for sacrifice was used for food. In general only the thigh bones, the entrails and some of the fat, was consumed on the altar, the remainder was eaten by priests, votaries, or attendants. In the case of the bloodless offerings, the cakes, fruit, grain, milk, wine, honey, &c., a large part also was used as food. A rule existed at Epidauros that all should be consumed within the precinct.

The so-called "Square building" marked K in the plan, may have been the scene both of minor sacrifices and of the consumption of the unsacrificed remnants. I have suggested above that this building might be a hostel, and the large quantities of ash, of bones, and of fragments of bronze and earthenware vessels found there to some extent support this hypothesis, and the idea that it was employed for the sacrificial banquets.

Among the hundreds of inscriptions found I have thus far only mentioned one class—namely, those referring to cures. There are, in addition, no fewer than thirteen other kinds of inscriptions; for example, the great poem of Isyllos, describing the genealogy and miracles of Asklepios, written by command of the oracle of Delphi. This has been edited and commented on in a most scholarly manner by Prof. von Wilamowitz-Möllendorff.

Many of the inscriptions are in honour of individual priests, pyrophoroi, hieromnemones, or of distinguished Greeks unconnected with the sanctuaries; for example there was found, in association with a headless statue, the inscription shown below.

Plate XXXII. The upper four lines of the inscription are in the Dorian dialect, the remainder in the Ionian. The former is the dedication of the statue by the Epidaurians to a historian previously unknown to the classical student, a certain Philippos of Pergamos. The lower Ionic fragment is probably a quotation (the only one known to exist) from his writings.

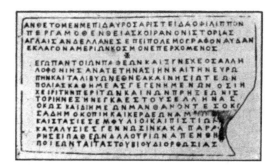

PLATE XXXII—Dedication of Statue to Philippos (Cavvadias)

Supplying the lost words or letters the inscription runs as follows :—

ἄνθετο μὲν μ' Ἐπίδαυρος Ἀριστείδαο Φίλιππον
Περγάμοθεν θείας κοίρανον ἱστορίας
ἀγλάϊσαν δ' Ἕλλανες ἐπεὶ πολεμογράφον αὐδὰν
ἔκλαγον ἀμερίων κόσμον ἐπερχόμενος.

*　　*　　*　　*

ἐγὼ παντοίων παθέων καὶ συνεχέος ἀλλη-
-λοφονίης ἀνά τε τὴν Ἀσίην καὶ τὴν Εὐρώ-
-πην καὶ τὰ Λιβύων ἔθνεα καὶ νησιωτέων
πόλιας καθ' ἡμέας γεγενημένων ὁσίῃ
χειρὶ τὴν περὶ τῶν καινῶν πρήξεων ἱσ-
-τορίην ἐξήνεγκα ἐς τοὺς Ἕλληνας
ὅκως καὶ δι' ἡμέων μανθάνοντες ὀκό-
-σα δημοκοπίη καὶ κερδέων ἀμ[ετρίαι]
καὶ στάσιες ἐμφύλιοι καὶ πιστίω[ν]
καταλύσιες γεννῶσιν κακὰ παρὰ [τῇ]
ῥήσει παθέων ἀλλοτρίων ἀπενθή[τως]
ποιέωνται τὰς τοῦ βίου διορθώσιας.

English Version.

"Set up in stone by Epidauros see,
A peerless scribe of god-like history,
Philip, the son of Aristeidas, come
Unto this holy place from Pergamum :
War was too long the theme of Greece ; my pen
Shrilled to ensue a peace for mortal men.

*　　*　　*　　*

" All sorts of suffering and endless bloodshed having taken place recently throughout Asia, Europe, the Libyan hordes, the island cities, I publish to the Greek world, without breach of trust, a 'History of our own Times,' in order that my countrymen may learn, by my means, what hosts of evils arise from political charlatanry and financial greed, quarrels in a nation, and acts of treachery, and so, by the recital of other people's miseries, may, without pain or grief to themselves, put their own lives in order, as occasions arise."

It is somewhat interesting to find the Boule of Epidauros thus doing special honour to a historian, and at the same time warning the Greek people against those political faults to which the nation was specially prone. The governing bodies of our health resorts do not show so large-minded an appreciation of letters or of political morals.*

A number of the later inscriptions are in honour of distinguished Romans.

There are numerous inscriptions regarding laws, or judicial decrees. Others, again, refer to the contests of the Stadium, while another and especially voluminous class relates to the construction of the temples and other buildings. In addition to the names of the architects and contractors, and the sums paid, these records contain many interesting details, *e.g.*, the statement that the pediment groups and acroteria on the temple of Asklepios were cut in marble by Hektoridas and another artificer, from models designed by the great sculptor Timotheus, the artist who, along with Scopas, designed parts of the mausoleum of Halicarnassus.

The minute details concerning the building of the Tholos, the amounts paid for marble and other materials, the names of architects and contractors, the report of the commissioners who inspected the work, and who formed a sort of lay buildings committee; their journeys to Athens, Corinth, Megara, and other places in quest of material, workmen, etc., the exact sums expended on these journeys, and other details, are curious and interesting. One can only regret that no hint is given of the use and purpose of the building on which so much care and thought were expended.

---

* An American friend suggests another explanation, viz., that the statue, although "set up by Epidauros," was paid for and the inscription inspired by Philippos of Pergamos himself. Though St. John, in the Apocalypse (II. 13) speaks unfavourably of that city ὅπου ὁ Σατανᾶς κατοικεῖ one feels unwilling to accuse one of its inhabitants of so astute a form of advertising.

I might occupy much time in showing and describing the
scores of sculptured votive tablets which have been recovered.
In most, of course, the figure of Asklepios has been destroyed
or damaged by the iconoclastic zeal of the early Christian.

In Plate XXXIII an almost uninjured example is shown.
A group of four suppliants with their children approach the
god, who leans on his staff with entwining serpent.   Behind
Asklepios is seen the head of (probably) his wife Epione, then

PLATE XXXIII—GROUP OF SUPPLIANTS APPROACHING ASKLEPIOS AND HIS FAMILY *

come Machaon and Podalirius, his sons, then, probably Hygieia,
Panakeia, and Iaso, his daughters.   The whole Asklepian family
are of heroic stature.

Every fourth year a great festival was held at the Hieron,
the Megala Asklepieia, at which athletic contests, races, processions, music, plays in the theatre, holy (perhaps also unholy)
vigils, lasting all night (especially if the Thracian Kotyttia
were enacted in the portico of Kotys), gorgeous rites, sacrifices,

* This slab has accidentally been reversed in the process of reproduction.

decoration of the temples and precincts, together with feasts, took place. Most probably the priests would arrange for the performance of a few miracles. Other festivals were also held, as the Megala Apolloneia.

On these occasions, if not at other times, doubtless every seat in the theatre, stadium, and hippodrome would be filled, mostly by sound and healthy visitors, coming, as I have suggested above, partly to enjoy a holiday, partly to witness athletic exercises, which interested them quite as much as important cricket, football, or rowing contests interest us, and partly to do honour to the god whose aid they might need when the days of sickness or old age should come.

Lastly, there is a link which, though of no practical import, is still a genuine historic bond connecting the Hieron of Epidauros with the medicine of Western Europe. Three centuries B.C. Rome was visited by dire pestilence. The rulers of Rome, having in vain endeavoured to check it, sought the counsel of the Sybilline books, and were directed to bring Asklepios to Rome from Epidauros. A galley was sent to the Saronic Gulf, and a mission visited the Hieron, bringing back to the ship one of the sacred serpents. The galley returned, entered the Tiber, approached Rome, and as it touched the insula in the Tiber the sacred serpent at once left the ship and found a refuge on the island. From that moment the plague is said to have rapidly disappeared.

In gratitude to the god, who was thus visibly among them in serpent form, the south end of the island—probably, indeed, the whole of the island—was modelled into the shape of a great galley of hewn stone. A temple of Æsculapius (as the Romans called him) was built at the southern end, with portico and abaton. A well existing there became sacred to Æsculapius, and from that day to this the island in the Tiber has, through pagan and Christian times alike, been devoted to the cure and treatment of the sick. The stern of the stone galley still exists, with the effigy of the serpent and remains of the image of Æsculapius. The Church of St. Bartholomew stands on the site of the temple, and on or near the spot where stood the ancient abaton now stands a hospital served by the Brotherhood of San Juan de Dios, the benevolent saint of Granada, where the sick folk of Rome are helped and tended; and there, unlike their predecessors of 2,200 years ago, if illness should terminate in death, the poor weary souls are kindly and tenderly ministered to by priest, physician, and nurse, until they sink into the last sleep.

It is doubtless in consequence of this episode of the founding of a temple of Æsculapius on the island of the Tiber that the staff and serpent of the Epidaurian god have been, and remain to this day, the symbol of the profession of Medicine.

LIST OF AUTHORITIES

Baunack (J.)   Aus Epidauros   1890
——————— (Ἐφημερίς, 1884)   1884
——————— Studien
——————— Zu den Inschriften aus Epidauros (*Philologus*,
    54)   1895
Blinkenberg (C.)   Asklepios og hans Frænder
——————— Inscriptions d'Epidaure (*Nordisk Tidsskrift for
    Filologi og Pædagogik*, 1895)   8°., Copenhagen, 1895
Brunn (.) Der Thron des Asklepios zu Epidauros (*Sitzungsb.
    der philosoph. philolog. u. histor. Classe d. k. b. Akad. der
    Wissensch. zu München*, 1872)   8°., München, 1872
Cavvadias (P.)   Δελτίον ἀρχαιολογικόν,   1891
——————— Ἐφημερὶς Ἀρχαιολογική,   1894
——————— Fouilles d'Epidaure, vol. i.   fo., Athènes, 1893
——————— Τὸ ἱερὸν τοῦ Ἀσκληπιοῦ ἐν Ἐπιδαύρῳ καὶ ἡ θεραπεία
    τῶν ἀσθενῶν.   8°., Athènes, 1900
——————— Inscriptions d'Epidaure (Ἐφημερὶς Ἀρχαιολογική,
    1883, 1886)   4°., Athènes, 1883-86
——————— Monuments d'Epidaure (Ἐφημερὶς Ἀρχαιολογική
    1884-85)
——————— Πρακτικὰ τῆς Ἀρχαιολ. Ἑταιρίας   1881-82-83-
    84, etc.
——————— Rapports sur les fouilles d'Epidaure (*Praktika*,
    1881-85)
Chipiez (C.)   (*Revue Archéologique*), 1896
Christ (W. von)   Das Theater des Polyklet in Epidauros
    (*Sitzungsb. der philosoph. philolog. u. histor. Classe d. k. b.
    Akad. der Wissensch. zu München*, 1894.)   8°., München,
                                                             1894
Defrasse (A.) and Lechat (H.)   Epidaure   fo., Paris, 1895
——————— Notes sur Epidaure (*Bulletin de Corresp. Hellénique*,
    1890)
Diehl (K.)   Excursions archéologiques en Grèce   1890

Diehl (K.) (*Athenische Mittheilungen*, 1893)
————— (*Berliner Philolog. Wochenschrift*, 1890)
Doerpfeld (W.) Der Rundbau in Epidauros (*Antike Denkmäler*, Bd. II, Heft I)   fo., Berlin, 1893
Dumon (K.) Le théâtre de Polyclite   4°., Paris, 1889
Foucart (P.) (*Bulletin de Corresp. Hellénique*, 14)   1890
————— Sur les sculptures et la date de quelques edifices d'Epidaure
Furtwaengler (A.) Epidauros (*Berliner Philolog. Wochenschrift*, 1888)
Gaidoz (H.) A propos des chiens d'Epidaure (*Revue Archéologique*, 3ᵉ série, 4)
Ganneau (C.) Esculape et le chien (*Revue Archéologique*, 1884)
Gardner (P.) New chapters in Greek history 8°., Lond., 1892
Girard (P.) L'Asklépieion d'Athènes d'après de récentes découvertes   1881
Herlich (S.) Epidaurus, eine Heilstätte   1898
Herold (.) (*Zeitschrift für Bauwesen*, 1893)
Kjellberg (L.) Asklepios. Mythologisch - archäologische Studien (*Särtryck ur Språkvetensk. Sällsk. förhandl.* 1894-97)
Koehler (G.) (*Athenische Mittheilungen*, 1877)
Koepp (F.) (*Athenische Mittheilungen*, 1885)
Merriam (A. C.) Dogs of Æsculapius (*American Antiquarian*, vol. 7)   Chicago, 1885
————— Marvellous cures at Epidauros (*American Antiquarian*, vol. 6)   Chicago, 1884
Panofka (T.) Asklepios und die Asklepiaden (*Abh. d. Berl. Akad.*, 1845)
Pausanius, *Periegetes*. Description of Greece, trans. with a commentary by J. G. Frazer 6 voll. ; 8°., Lond., 1898
————— Mythology and monuments of ancient Athens, being a trans. of the *Attica* of Pausanias by M. de Verrall, with intro. by J. E. Harrison   8°., Lond., 1890
Petersen (C.) Athenastatuen von Epidauros (*Mitth.*, vol. xi)
Reinach (S.) Les chiens dans le culte d'Esculape (*Revue Archéologique*, 1884)
————— Chronique d'Orient (*Revue Archéologique*, 1884)
————— La seconde stèle des guérisons miraculeuses (*Revue Archéologique*, 1885)

49

Staïs (V.) Ἐφημερίς. 1892
———————— Monuments d'Epidaure (Ἐφημερὶς Ἀρχαιολογική,
    1886)
Vercoutre (.)   (*Revue Archéologique*, 1884-85)
Walton (A.)   The cult of Asklepios   (*Cornell Studies*, No. III)
Wilamowitz-Möllendorff (U. von)   Isyllus von Epidaurus

For EU product safety concerns, contact us at Calle de José Abascal, 56–1°,
28003 Madrid, Spain or eugpsr@cambridge.org.

www.ingramcontent.com/pod-product-compliance
Ingram Content Group UK Ltd.
Pitfield, Milton Keynes, MK11 3LW, UK
UKHW030856150625
459647UK00021B/2787